"Be careful with this dynamite book. It may explode into your life and you will never be the same. It's a message that brings the most important truths of God's Word into balance. Don't just read it—give copies to your friends!"

GEORGE VERWER,
FOUNDER OF OPERATION MOBILIZATION

"I didn't merely read *The Grace and Truth Paradox*, I drank it down like a thirsty woman who'd discovered a deep well of fresh, clean water. This book overflows with grace *and* truth, carefully presenting a case for both elements to co-exist in the hearts and lives of believers. I found myself whispering, 'Yes! Yes! ' as I read, underlining like mad and committing to memory the important truths and grace-filled examples that fill the pages of this refreshing book."

LIZ CURTIS HIGGS, BESTSELLING AUTHOR OF
BAD GIRLS OF THE BIBLE

"Reading a Randy Alcorn book is like opening a treasure chest. Within these pages you'll discover truth seasoned with grace and presented with excellence."

HANK HANEGRAAFF, HOST OF THE SYNDICATED
RADIO PROGRAM *THE BIBLE ANSWER MAN*

"In his probing, incisive manner, Randy Alcorn presses us to examine our lives for any lack of balance. He paints a compelling picture of what it means to walk as Christ did, in both grace and truth."

NANCY LEIGH DEMOSS,
HOST OF *REVIVE OUR HEARTS*
AND AUTHOR OF *LIES WOMEN BELIEVE*

"In this marvelous and very readable book, Randy Alcorn clearly illustrates how grace and truth are not opposites, but are both essential to loving our neighbors."

BILL BRIGHT, FOUNDER, CAMPUS CRUSADE
FOR CHRIST INTERNATIONAL

"Read this book carefully, prayerfully, and meditatively. Listen for God's still small voice to speak. Heed the warnings and expectantly look forward to Christ's grace and truth, in balance, dramatically changing your world."

WALT LARIMORE, VICE PRESIDENT OF
MEDICAL OUTREACH, FOCUS ON THE FAMILY

"For all of us who desire to understand concretely and simply the essence of being like Jesus, this book is a must-read."

JOSEPH M. STOWELL, PRESIDENT, MOODY BIBLE
INSTITUTE AND AUTHOR OF *SIMPLY JESUS*

The GRACE and TRUTH PARADOX

LifeChange Books

RANDY ALCORN

Multnomah Books

THE GRACE AND TRUTH PARADOX
published by Multnomah Books

© 2003 by Eternal Perspective Ministries
International Standard Book Number: 978-1-59052-065-9

Cover image © Somerset House Publishing, Inc., Nancy Glazier 2002

Unless otherwise indicated, Scripture quotations are from:
The Holy Bible, New International Version © 1973, 1984
by International Bible Society, used by permission of Zondervan Publishing House
Other Scripture quotations:

New American Standard Bible® (NASB) © 1960, 1977, 1995 by the Lockman Foundation.
The Holy Bible, New King James Version (NKJV) © 1984 by Thomas Nelson, Inc.

Published in the United States by WaterBrook Multnomah, an imprint of the Crown
Publishing Group, a division of Random House Inc., New York.

MULTNOMAH and its mountain colophon are registered trademarks of Random House Inc.

Printed in the United States of America

For information:
MULTNOMAH BOOKS • 12265 ORACLE BOULEVARD, SUITE 200
COLORADO SPRINGS, CO 80921

Library of Congress Cataloging-in-Publication Data
Alcorn, Randy C.
  The grace and truth paradox / by Randy Alcorn.
    p. cm.
  Includes bibliographical references.
  Contents: A two-point checklist of Christlikeness—Essential and inseparable—What is
grace?—What is truth?—A closer look at grace—A closer look at truth—The grace we long
for—The truth that sets us free—Grace and truth together.
  ISBN 1-59052-065-3
    1. Christian life. 2. Grace (Theology) 3. Truth (Christian theology) 4. Bible. N.T. John I
14—Critricism, interpretation, etc. I. Title.
BV4501.3 .A519 2003
248.4—dc21

                                        2002014114

11 12 13—15 14 13

Dedication

To Laura Libby,
who lives now
in the Land of
Grace and Truth

Contents

Acknowledgments

The author wishes to acknowledge his friend and editor, Larry Libby:

Thanks, Larry, for being a better editor than anyone deserves and for being a man so characterized by grace and truth.

Chapter 1

A TWO-POINT CHECKLIST OF CHRISTLIKENESS

Late one rainy night, my wife and I were leaving a movie theater when Nanci noticed an older man in the parking lot leaning on a walker, struggling. I helped him get into his car. Since he was so exhausted, I asked if I could drive him home.

He declined, but I said we'd follow him home in case he needed help. As he pulled out, driving erratically, we prayed he wouldn't find the street. Our prayers were answered when he got trapped in a fast-food drive-through line. I opened his door and asked him to move to the passenger seat so I could drive him home, while Nanci followed.

As I pulled out, two men jumped in front of the car, waving their arms and a cell phone. One shouted, "My wife's having our baby, and I have to get home. Can you drive us?"

"Well," I said, "this isn't my car, and I don't know this man sitting next to me."

Sounded pretty lame, don't you think?

I asked Nanci to drive the older man's car and follow me while I took those guys home (wherever that was). After dropping them off, I hopped back in with George—by now I knew his name—to take him home (wherever that was). When we reached his place, I helped him to his room.

I found out George had been a political science professor at San Francisco State University for twenty-eight years. I realized that most people of George's background would not count Bible-believing Christians among their favorite people! George asked me why we had helped him. I told him we were followers of Christ. I left him my book *In Light of Eternity.* I prayed God would touch his life and hoped we'd hear the rest of the story in eternity.

As it turns out, we didn't have to wait that long.

Two months later my assistant Kathy woke up in the middle of the night experiencing a strange medical problem she'd never had before and hasn't had since. The next day she went to her doctor, bringing with her a copy of *In Light of Eternity.* When the doctor saw it, he said, "One of my patients was carrying that book the other day—and he told me he wished he could talk to the author."

Kathy returned to our office with George's phone number. I called him and asked if he wanted me to drop by. He did. George was full of questions. He wanted to know the truth about Jesus Christ. He couldn't get over the idea of grace, that God could really forgive rotten people. He said it sounded "too easy."

Two hours of discussion followed. I saw God's Spirit at work in George. Finally he prayed, confessed his sin, and accepted Christ's gift of eternal life.

Now, what are the chances of all these events coinciding?

No chance at all—they were a series of divine appointments.

A small act of grace by my wife and me (two small acts, counting the trip to the woman ready to deliver a baby) somehow made an impression on George—and also got into his hands a book that offered him the truth.

What George saw, what he wrestled with, and what ultimately brought him to Christ was grace and truth.

WHAT GIVES US AWAY?

A friend sat down in a small London restaurant and picked up a menu.

"What will it be?" the waiter asked.

Studying the puzzling selections, my friend said, "Uhh…"

The waiter smiled. "Oh, a Yank. What part of the States are you from?"

He hadn't said a word. But he'd already given himself away.

In the first century, Christ's followers were also recognized immediately. What gave them away?

It wasn't their buildings. They had none.

It wasn't their programs. They had none.

It wasn't their political power. They had none.

It wasn't their slick publications, TV networks, bumper stickers, or celebrities. They had none.

What was it?

With great power the apostles continued to testify
to the resurrection of the Lord Jesus, and much
grace was upon them all.

ACTS 4:33

They testified to the truth about Christ and lived by His grace. Truth was the food they ate and the message they spoke. Grace was the air they breathed and the life they lived.

The world around them had never seen anything like it. It still hasn't.

THE TWO ESSENTIALS

The only "church growth formula" the early church pos-
sessed was the body of truth flowing with the blood of
grace. They drew thousands to Jesus by being like Jesus.

But what does it mean to "be like Jesus"? We could
come up with long lists of His character qualities. But the
longer the list, the less we can wrap our minds around it. (I
can't even juggle three balls. How could I juggle dozens?)

But what if the character of Christ was reducible to two
ingredients?

In fact, it is:

> In the beginning was the Word, and the Word was
> with God, and the Word was God.... The Word
> became flesh and made his dwelling among us. We
> have seen his glory, the glory of the One and Only,
> who came from the Father, *full of grace and truth.*

JOHN 1:1, 14, EMPHASIS ADDED

Jesus is full of two things: grace and truth.

Not "full of patience, wisdom, beauty, compassion, and
creativity." In the list there are no commas and only one
conjunction—grace *and* truth. Scripture distills Christ's
attributes into a two-point checklist of Christlikeness.

The baby born in a Bethlehem barn was Creator of the
universe. He pitched His tent on the humble camping
ground of our little planet. God's glory no longer dwelt in

a temple of wood and stone, but in Christ. He was the Holy of Holies.

But when He ascended back into the wide blue heavens, He left God's shekinah glory—that visible manifestation of God's presence—on earth. We Christians became His living temples, the new Holy of Holies (1 Corinthians 3:16–17; 6:19).

People had only to look at Jesus to see what God is like. *People today should only have to look at us to see what Jesus is like.* For better or worse, they'll draw conclusions about Christ from what they see in us. If we fail the grace test, we fail to be Christlike. If we fail the truth test, we fail to be Christlike. If we pass both tests, we're like Jesus.

A grace-starved, truth-starved world needs Jesus, full of grace and truth.

So what does this hungry world see when it looks at us?

SURPRISED BY GRACE

First-century Jewish culture understood truth far better than grace. Grace comes first in John 1:14 because it was more *surprising*.

When Jesus stepped onto the world's stage, people could not only hear the demands of truth but also see Truth Himself. No longer fleeting glimmers of grace, but Grace Himself. "Behold, the Lamb of God who takes away the sin of the world" (John 1:29, NASB).

When God passed in front of Moses, He identified Himself as "abounding in love and faithfulness" (Exodus 34:6). The words translated *love* and *faithfulness* are the Hebrew equivalents of *grace* and *truth*.

Grace is a delightful, fragrant word.

It intrigues.

Attracts.

Compels.

Dazzles.

It also confounds. It's as though God said, "You know about truth. It's taught in synagogues every Sabbath. But let Me tell you about grace…"

The Old Testament teaches the fear of God, spelling out the horrendous consequences of disregarding truth. It presents truth relentlessly. Uzzah was struck down for simply steadying the ark of the covenant with his hand.

There's certainly grace in the Old Testament—lots of it—but it was overshadowed by truth. The Pharisees, God's self-appointed gatekeepers, never emphasized grace. Christ's hearers had seen truth in the law of Moses, but it was Christ who gave them their first clear view of grace. The law could only reveal sin. Jesus could *remove* it.

Some churches today embrace truth but need *a heavy dose of grace.*

Other churches talk about grace but cry out for *a heavy dose of truth.*

Some time ago, I invited a lesbian activist to lunch. For the first hour, she hammered me, telling of all the Christians who'd mistreated her. She seemed as hard as nails. I listened, trying to show her God's grace, praying she'd see the Jesus she desperately needed. She raised her voice and cursed freely. People stared. But that was okay. Jesus went to the cross for her—the least I could do was listen.

Suddenly she was crying, sobbing, broken. I reached across the table and took her hand. For the next two hours I heard her story, her heartsickness, her doubts about the causes she championed. I told her about Christ's grace.

After four hours we walked out of that restaurant, side by side. We hugged.

In our conversation, truth wasn't shared at the expense of grace, or grace at the expense of truth.

Birds need two wings to fly. With only one wing, they're grounded. The gospel flies with the wings of grace and truth. Not one, but both.

ACHIEVING BALANCE

The apparent conflict that exists between grace and truth isn't because they're incompatible, but because we lack perspective to resolve their paradox. The two are *interdependent*. We should never approach truth except in a spirit of grace, or grace except in a spirit of truth. Jesus wasn't 50 percent grace, 50 percent truth, but 100 percent grace, 100 percent truth.

Truth-oriented Christians love studying Scripture and theology. But sometimes they're quick to judge and slow to forgive. They're strong on truth, weak on grace.

Grace-oriented Christians love forgiveness and freedom. But sometimes they neglect Bible study and see moral standards as "legalism." They're strong on grace, weak on truth.

Countless mistakes in marriage, parenting, ministry, and other relationships are failures to balance grace and truth. Sometimes we neglect both. Often we choose one over the other.

It reminds me of Moses, our dalmatian.

When one tennis ball is in his mouth, the other's on the floor. When he goes for the second ball, he drops the first. Large dogs can get two balls in their mouth. Not Moses. He manages to get two in his mouth only momentarily. To his distress, one ball or the other spurts out onto the floor.

Similarly, our minds don't seem big enough to hold on to grace *and* truth at the same time. We go after the grace ball— only to drop the truth ball to make room for it. We need to stretch our undersized minds to hold them both at once.

A paradox is an *apparent* contradiction. Grace and truth aren't really contradictory. Jesus didn't switch on truth and then turn it off so He could switch on grace. Both are permanently switched on in Jesus. Both should be switched on in us.

What would Jesus do? There is always one answer: He would act in grace and truth.

Truth without grace breeds a self-righteous legalism that poisons the church and pushes the world away from Christ.

Grace without truth breeds moral indifference and keeps people from seeing their need for Christ.

Attempts to "soften" the gospel by minimizing truth keep people from Jesus. Attempts to "toughen" the gospel by minimizing grace keep people from Jesus. It's not enough for us to offer grace *or* truth.

We must offer both.

That's what this little book is all about.

Chapter 2

ESSENTIAL AND INSEPARABLE

Most sinners loved being around Jesus. They enjoyed His company, sought Him out, invited Him to their homes and parties. Today most sinners don't want to be around Christians. Unbelievers tore off the roof to get to Jesus. Sometimes they crawl out the windows to get away from us!

Why is that? What did Jesus show them that we don't? Grace.

People sensed that Jesus loved them, even when He spoke difficult words. He was full of grace *and* truth. He drew them out of the night like a light draws moths.

Some church services are permeated with Christian clichés that mystify unbelievers. Nobody's drawn to what's incomprehensible. Grace compels us to put the cookies of truth on the lower shelf where the uninitiated can reach them. Jesus warmly welcomed the nonreligious and spoke words they understood. So should we.

Other churches try to make sinners feel comfortable. How? They never talk about sin. Never offend anyone. They replace truth with tolerance, lowering the bar so everyone can jump over it and we can all feel good about ourselves.

But Jesus said, "'No servant is greater than his master.' If they persecuted me, they will persecute you also" (John 15:20).

Something's wrong if all unbelievers hate us.

Something's wrong if all unbelievers like us.

If we accurately demonstrate grace *and* truth, some will be drawn to us and others will be offended by us—just as they were by Jesus.

When we offend everybody, it's because we've taken on the truth mantle without grace. When we offend nobody, it's because we've watered down truth in the name of grace.

STAYING IN THE SADDLE

When a musical instrument's strings go loose, it sounds awful. But you can also overtighten the strings, breaking them or creating discord. There's a perfect tension to grace and truth, which makes the gospel's music.

Martin Luther said that the devil doesn't care which side of the horse we fall off of—as long as we don't stay in the saddle. We need to ride the horse with one foot in the stirrup of truth, the other in the stirrup of grace.

In *The Lion, the Witch and the Wardrobe*, Susan asks Mr. and Mrs. Beaver about Aslan the Lion:

> "Is he—quite safe? I shall feel rather nervous about meeting a lion."
>
> "That you will dearie, and no mistake," said Mrs. Beaver. "If there's anyone who can appear before Aslan without their knees knocking, they're either braver than most or just plain silly."
>
> "Then he isn't safe?" said Lucy.
>
> "Safe?" said Mr. Beaver; "don't you hear what Mrs. Beaver tells you? Who said anything about safe? Of course he isn't safe. But he's good. He's the King, I tell you."[1]

Christ is good. But until we understand that He's not "safe," until we come to grips with the truth of His uncompromising holiness, we'll never begin to grasp His grace.

Many today try to reinvent Jesus, giving Him a facelift. They spin His statements for public consumption, making Him fit popular notions of the kind of Christ people want. But He's notoriously uncooperative with all attempts to repackage and market Him. He's not looking for image-enhancers. We're to follow Him as servants, not walk in front of Him as a PR entourage.

When Jesus walked this earth, many people didn't recognize Him. They were looking for the Messiah as a powerful lion, bringing judgment on His enemies. But they overlooked the passages showing Him coming as a lamb:

> He was oppressed and afflicted,
>   yet he did not open his mouth;
> he was led like a lamb to the slaughter,
>   and as a sheep before her shearers is silent,
> so he did not open his mouth.

ISAIAH 53:7

The lamb appears "looking as if it had been slain" (Revelation 5:6). This seems a picture of weakness. But suddenly men are hiding themselves from the "wrath of the Lamb" (6:16). "They will make war against the Lamb, but the Lamb will overcome them because he is Lord of lords and King of kings" (17:14).

At the end of *The Voyage of the Dawn Treader*, the children see a bright white lamb, speaking in a "sweet milky voice." As they talk, suddenly "his snowy white flushed into tawny gold and his size changed and he was Aslan himself, towering above them and scattering light from his mane."[2] The lamb of grace is the lion of truth.

Sometimes we see Him as one, sometimes the other. Always He is both.

SPIRITUAL SYMMETRY

DNA's double helix is perfect balance at life's core. Two strands of DNA wrap around each other, an axis of symmetry. The two strands run opposite directions, providing perfect correction for each other.

Grace and truth are spiritual DNA, the building blocks of Christ-centered living. These complementary strands create flawless spiritual balance and stability. Though the strands run opposite directions, they correspond perfectly. Without both strands we cannot properly function.

The trick is finding that perfect balance. It isn't always easy. Believe me, I know.

In 1989 and 1990 I intervened, peacefully and nonviolently, at abortion clinics on behalf of unborn children. As a result I was arrested several times and sent to jail for a few days.

I don't regret what I did; I still believe that unborn children are precious to their Creator. That truth compelled me to say and do things that proved unpopular—among non-Christians and Christians alike. What got me in trouble was attempting to honor both truth and grace.

I asked myself, if these really are children—not just *potential* children—don't they need people to "speak up for those who cannot speak for themselves.... Defend the rights of the poor and needy" (Proverbs 31:8–9)?

I felt compelled to show grace to unbelievers. I never shouted, jeered, or demeaned. I never raised my voice, touched anyone, or said anything unkind. Alongside others, I sought to share Christ's grace at abortion clinics. (One person came to Christ right outside the clinic door.)

A few years ago, the church I used to pastor (and still attend) was picketed by thirty protestors. Why? Some of our people go to abortion clinics and offer alternatives, sharing the gospel when they can. Sometimes they hold up signs saying, "Consider Adoption," "Let Your Baby Live," or "We'll Help Financially."

Three proabortion groups decided to join forces and give our church "a taste of our own medicine." On a rainy Sunday morning, our church parking lot was invaded by Radical Women for Choice, Rock for Choice, and the Lesbian Avengers. Having heard they were coming, we set out doughnuts and coffee. I spent an hour and a half with a protestor named Charles, who held a sign that said, "Keep Abortion Legal."

We talked a little about abortion and a lot about Christ. I explained the gospel. He gave me his address. Later I sent him some of my books and some Christian literature.

I liked Charles. But when you believe as I do that abortion is killing children, it's a bit awkward serving coffee and holding an umbrella for someone waving a proabortion sign. If you don't understand, imagine doing that for someone holding a sign declaring, "Legalize Rape" or "Kill Blacks."

Yet because of the opportunity to share Christ's grace, it seemed right.

But it's not just truth that puts us in awkward situations. Grace does too. On the morning we were picketed, some street preachers with signs shouting hell and damnation showed up to take on the abortion activists. Their message contained truth, but their approach lacked grace. One of the street preachers barged between my daughter and me and a few of the Lesbian Avengers just as we finally had an opportunity to talk with them. The door of witnessing was slammed in our faces...by Christian brothers.

We tried to reason with the street preachers. After all, this was our church, and we didn't want them screaming at our "guests"—even if they were screaming truth. Most cooperated, but a few decided we were waffling on truth and it was an abomination for us to offer doughnuts to people who needed to be rebuked.

The following Sunday two street preachers picketed our church, scolding us for our "pathetic" attempts at doughnut and coffee evangelism.

So after twenty-one unpicketed years, our church was picketed two weeks in a row! First, by radically liberal nonbelievers, for speaking truth. Second, by radically conservative believers, for showing grace.

That's how it is on this tightrope walk between truth and grace. When you stand for truth, you're held in contempt by some non-Christians (and even some Christians). When you try to demonstrate grace, you're held in contempt by some Christians (and even some non-Christians). When you try to live by grace and truth, in some eyes you'll be too radical, in other eyes not radical enough.

Some people hate truth. Others hate grace. Jesus loves both. We can't undercut either without undercutting Him.

So we have to make a choice. Are we going to spend our lives trying to please the grace-haters or the truth-haters? Or are we going to seek to please the only One whose judgment seat we'll stand before: Jesus, who is full of grace and truth?

Chapter 3

WHAT IS GRACE?

Nanci and I spent an unforgettable day in England with Phil and Margaret Holder. Margaret was born in China to missionary parents with China Inland Mission. In 1939, when Japan took control of eastern China, thirteen-year-old Margaret was imprisoned in a Japanese internment camp. There she remained, separated from her parents, for six years.

Margaret told us stories about a godly man called "Uncle Eric." He tutored her and was deeply loved by all the children in the camp. We were amazed to discover that "Uncle Eric" was Eric Liddell, "The Flying Scot," hero of the movie *Chariots of Fire*. Liddell shocked the world by refusing to run the one hundred meters in the 1924 Paris Olympics, a race he was favored to win. He withdrew because the qualifying heat was on a Sunday.

Liddell won a gold medal—and broke a world record—in the four hundred meters, not his strongest event. Later he went as a missionary to China. When war broke out, he sent his pregnant wife and his daughters to safety. Imprisoned by the Japanese, he never saw his family in this world again. Suffering with a brain tumor, Eric Liddell died in 1945, shortly after his forty-third birthday.

Through fresh tears, Margaret told us, "It was a cold February day when Uncle Eric died."

At times it seemed unbearable to be cut off from their homes and families. But Margaret spoke with delight of "care packages falling from the sky"—barrels of food and supplies dropped from American planes.

One day Margaret and the other children were lined up as usual to count off for roll call. Suddenly an American airplane flew low. They watched it circle and drop more of those wonderful food barrels. But as the barrels came near the ground, the captives realized something was different. Her eyes bright, Margaret told us, "This time the barrels had legs!" The sky was full of American soldiers, parachuting down to rescue them.

Margaret and several hundred children rushed out of the camp, past Japanese guards who offered no resistance. Free for the first time in six years, they ran to the soldiers that were raining down everywhere. They threw themselves on their rescuers, hugging and kissing them.

Imagine the children's joy. Imagine the *soldiers'* joy.

God rejoices in the grace He offers us as much as we rejoice in receiving it. Whether it's Him returning from the sky to liberate us, or drawing us to Himself through our deaths, we will be rescued and at last reunited with loved ones who've gone before us. We'll be taken home.

THE COST OF GRACE

Hounded by the Pharisees, betrayed by a friend, forsaken by His disciples, brutalized by police, beaten by His inquisitors, led in disgrace to a rigged trial.

Arrogant men sitting in judgment over Him, crowning Him with thorns, mocking and disdaining. Beating Him without mercy, nailing Him to the cross, the worst of tortures, stretched out between thieves.

Miserably thirsty, utterly forsaken by His Father for the first time, the picture of complete aloneness.

Hell on earth! Not just one man's hell, but the hell of billions. At any moment—in a millisecond—He could have called legions of angels to deliver Him and destroy His enemies. Instead, He bears forever the scars of sin, rebellion, mockery, and hatred…the scars of God's grace.

The cost of redemption cannot be overstated. The wonders of grace cannot be overemphasized. Christ took the hell He didn't deserve so we could have the heaven we don't deserve.

If you're not stunned by the thought of grace, then you aren't grasping what grace offers you, or what it cost Jesus.

In 1987, eighteen-month-old "Baby Jessica" fell twenty-two feet into a Texas well. Rescuers labored nonstop to save her. After fifty-five grueling hours, her life hanging in the balance, they finally reached her and extracted her from the well. The nation breathed a sigh of relief and cheered the heroes.

This was *not* the story: "Baby Jessica clawed her eighteen-month-old body up the side of that twenty-two foot well, inch by inch, digging in her little toes and working her way up. She's a hero, that Jessica!"

Baby Jessica was utterly helpless. She could do nothing to deliver herself. Her fate was in the hands of her rescuers. Left to herself, Jessica had no chance. Likewise, when it comes to our salvation, we're utterly powerless. That's grace: "At just the right time, when we were still powerless, Christ died for the ungodly" (Romans 5:6).

We get no more applause for our redemption than Baby Jessica got for being rescued. God alone deserves the ovation. In the story of redemption, He's the only hero. And it didn't just cost Him fifty-five hours of hard work— it cost Him everything.

Do you want to say "Thank You" right now?

A WRETCH LIKE WHO?

Before I spoke at a conference, a soloist sang one of my favorite songs, "Amazing Grace."

It was beautiful. Until she got to the tenth word.

"Amazing grace! How sweet the sound that saved a *soul* like me!"

My heart sank. The word *wretch* had been edited out! I thought about John Newton, the songwriter. This former slave trader, guilty of the vilest sins, *knew* he was a wretch. And that's what made God's grace so "amazing." Mind-boggling. Knockdown awesome.

If we're nothing more than morally neutral "souls," do you see what that does? It guts grace. The better we are, the less we need it. The less amazing it becomes. (Change the Baby Jessica story to rescuing Osama bin Laden and you have a better picture of redemption.)

The Bible makes an astounding proclamation: "God demonstrates his own love for us in this: While we were still sinners, Christ died for us" (Romans 5:8).

When you cut wretch *out of the song, you shrink grace.* You reduce it to something more sensible, less surprising. If we weren't so bad without Christ, why did He have to endure the cross? Paul said if men were good enough, then "Christ died for nothing" (Galatians 2:21).

Grace never ignores the awful truth of our depravity. In

fact, it emphasizes it. The worse we realize we are, the greater we realize God's grace is.

Grace isn't about God lowering His standards. It's about God fulfilling those standards through the substitutionary suffering of the standard-setter. Christ went to the cross because He would not ignore the truths of His holiness and our sin. Grace never ignores or violates truth. Grace gave what truth demanded: the ultimate sacrifice for our sins.

For some, human depravity may be an insulting doctrine, but grasping it is liberating. Why? Because when I realize that the best I can do without Him is like "filthy rags" in His sight (Isaiah 64:6), it finally sinks in that I have nothing to offer. Salvation therefore hinges on His work, not mine.

You and I, after all, weren't (or aren't, if you don't yet know Him) merely sick in our sins; we were *dead* in our sins (Ephesians 2:1–3). That means I'm not just unworthy of salvation; I'm utterly incapable of earning it. Corpses can't raise themselves from the grave.

What relief to realize that my salvation cannot be earned by good works—and therefore can't be lost by bad ones.

If we see God as He really is, and ourselves as we really are, there's only one appropriate response: to worship Him. I once heard someone say, "Only the humble are sane." I have to agree. Humility isn't pretending that we're unworthy because it's the spiritual thing to do; it's recognizing that we're unworthy *because it's true.*

GRACE AND GRATITUDE

"Who has ever given to God, that God should repay him?" (Romans 11:35). The answer is *nobody*.

Our culture is riddled with a poisonous spirit of entitlement. We always think we deserve more. We're disappointed with our family, neighbors, church, the waitress, the sales clerk, and the department of motor vehicles. Ultimately we're disappointed with God. He hasn't given us everything we want.

What madness! If only we could see our situation clearly—even for a moment. We deserved expulsion; He gives us a diploma. We deserved the electric chair; He gives us a parade. Anything less than overwhelming gratitude should be unthinkable. He owes us nothing. We owe Him everything. When you realize you deserve nothing better than hell, it puts a "bad day" in perspective, doesn't it?

Christians in Sudan—who've suffered unspeakably for their faith—are deeply grateful for God's daily blessings. But us? We whine and pout.

Thankfulness should draw a clear line between us and a Christless world. If the same spirit of entitlement and ingratitude that characterizes our culture characterizes us, what do we have to offer?

If I grasp that I deserve hell, I'll be filled with gratitude not only for God's huge blessings—including my redemption and home in heaven—but also for His smaller blessings: sun, rain, a beating heart, eyes that see, legs that walk, a mind that thinks. If I *don't* have these, I'll be overwhelmed with the knowledge that I have plenty else I don't deserve. And because Christ allowed Himself to be crushed under the weight of my sin, I'll enjoy forever a clear mind and perfect body.

Imagine a great and generous king. In the midst of his benevolent reign, he hears that his subjects have revolted. He sends messengers to investigate. The rebels kill them. So he sends his own dear son, the prince. They murder him viciously, hanging his body on the city wall.

What would you expect the king to do now? Send his armies and take revenge, right? *Kill those rebels! Burn their villages to ashes!* That king certainly has both the power and the right to avenge himself.

But what if the king turned around and offered these criminals a full pardon?

"I will accept my son—whom you murdered—as the payment for all your rebellion. You may go free. All I require is for you to admit your transgressions and embrace my son's purchase of your forgiveness."

We'd be stunned—blown away—to hear this, wouldn't we? But the king's not finished.

"I invite any of you to come live in my palace, eat at my table, and enjoy all the pleasures of my kingdom. And I will adopt you as my own children and make you my heirs, so everything that's mine will be yours forever."

Incredible.

Then he says, "I won't force you to accept my offer. But the only alternative is spending the rest of your life in prison. The choice is yours."

Can you imagine someone responding, "How *dare* the king send anyone to prison? What a cruel tyrant!"?

This is God's grace to us. If trying to comprehend it doesn't stretch your brain, you just aren't getting it.

Because grace is so incomprehensible to us, we bootleg in conditions so we won't look so bad and God's offer won't seem so counterintuitive. By the time we're done qualifying the gospel, we're no longer unworthy and powerless. We're "misguided souls." We're no longer wretches. And grace is no longer grace.

The worst thing we can teach people is that they're good without Jesus. The fact is, God doesn't offer grace to good people any more than doctors offer lifesaving surgery to healthy people. Jesus said, "It is not the healthy who need a doctor, but the sick. I have not come to call the righteous, but sinners to repentance" (Luke 5:31–32).

Never believe anything about yourself or God that makes His grace to you seem anything less than astonishing.

Because that's exactly what it is.

Chapter 4

WHAT IS TRUTH?

Marty, a businessman in our home Bible study, described how his boss made promises to customers that the company couldn't honor. Our group suggested he confront his boss. If the man wouldn't change his business ethics, Marty should resign.

It felt risky to encourage Marty to take a stand for truth. After all, though a nice guy, he wasn't a believer. We might reason, "Let's not impose truth on Marty. He just needs to hear about grace."

The next day Marty called me. "Listening to the group made me realize that you have something I really need." So we met for lunch. I shared with him about the One who's full of grace and truth. We bowed our heads; Marty repented of his sins and right there in that restaurant booth gave his life to Christ.

God used the persuasive power of Christian truth, graciously explained by people in our Bible study. Marty was led to grace by the truth.

THE GUARDRAILS OF TRUTH

Godly living centers not on what we avoid, but on whom we embrace. Anytime we talk more about dos and don'ts than about Jesus, something's wrong.

The Christian life is far more than sin management. *Behavior modification that's not empowered by God's heart-changing grace is self-righteous, as repugnant to God as the worst sins people gossip about.* Children who grow up with graceless truth are repelled by self-righteousness and attracted to the world's slickly marketed grace-substitutes.

The world's low standards, its disregard for truth, are not grace. The illusory freedom, however, *feels* like grace to someone who's been pounded by graceless truth—beaten over the head with a piece of the guardrail. In fact, people who grow up in joyless religion learn that there's no hope of living up to such daunting standards. "Why even try? It's *impossible!*"

But properly understood, biblical truths are guardrails that protect us from plunging off the cliff. A smart traveler doesn't curse the guardrails. He doesn't whine, "That guardrail dented my fender!" He looks over the cliff, sees demolished autos below, and is *grateful* for guardrails.

The guardrails of truth are there not to punish, but to protect us.

DEFINING TRUTH

Jesus prayed, "Sanctify them by the truth; your word is truth" (John 17:17).

Truth is more than mere facts. It's not just something we act upon. It acts upon us. We cannot change the truth, but the truth can change us. It sanctifies (sets us apart) from the falsehoods woven into our sin nature and championed by the world.

God has written His truth on human hearts (Romans 2:15). Shame and twinges of conscience come from recognizing that truth has been violated. When people hear truth spoken graciously, many are drawn to it because of the moral vacuum they feel. Hearts long for truth—even hearts that reject it.

We are to walk in the truth (3 John 1:3), love the truth, and believe the truth (2 Thessalonians 2:10, 12). All truth has a center of gravity: Jesus Christ, who declared, "I am the way and the truth and the life" (John 14:6). He didn't say He would show the truth or teach the truth or model the truth. He *is* the truth. Truth personified. He's the source of truth, and the reference point for evaluating all truth-claims.

That's why if we get it wrong about Jesus, it doesn't matter what else we get right.

"The God of truth" (Psalm 31:5) is "not a man, that he should lie, nor a son of man, that he should change his mind" (Numbers 23:19).

The devil is a con man, always denying, revising, and spinning the truth, rearranging the price tags. Jesus said, "There is no truth in him." He called him a "liar and the father of lies." He said, "When he lies, he speaks his native language" (John 8:44). Satan is a natural when it comes to deception. He's eloquent. Smooth. Persuasive. Believable. And we are so gullible.

When we speak the truth, we speak Christ's language. When we speak lies, we speak Satan's language.

You and I can discover truth, but we cannot create it. What's true is true and what's not is not—for all of us, all the time. Our culture views truth as something *inside* us, subject to revision according to our growth and enlightenment. Scripture views truth as something *outside* us, which we can believe or not but can never sway.

Truth isn't about our own perceptions or desires. It's always about Reality, with a capital *R*. A majority of us could agree that we'd like gravity to be suspended tomorrow, but our vote would have no impact on reality. Americans embrace democratic ideals. This gives us the illusion that we should have a voice when it comes to truth. But the universe isn't a democracy. Truth isn't a ballot measure.

We easily confuse what we *want* to be true with what

actually *is* true. C. S. Lewis said he wrote to expound mere Christianity, "which is what it is and was what it was long before I was born and whether I like it or not."³

All of us have a theology. The only question is whether it's true or false. Much teaching today is popularity-driven, not truth-driven. "The time will come when men will not put up with sound doctrine. Instead, to suit their own desires, they will gather around them a great number of teachers to say what their itching ears want to hear" (2 Timothy 4:3).

Some pastors and television preachers are well paid to play fast and loose with truth. But Charles Spurgeon said, "Christ's people must have bold, unflinching lion-like hearts, loving Christ first, and His truth next, and Christ and His truth beyond all the world."⁴

We should take our cues from the Berean Christians, who "received the message with great eagerness and examined the Scriptures every day" to determine whether what they were being taught was true (Acts 17:11).

TRUTH 101: IS JESUS THE ONLY WAY?

The most influential theologian in America may be Oprah Winfrey. Her "spirituality" is a hodgepodge of psychology, recovery, and out-of-context Scripture. The Oprah way is a church-free, build-it-yourself spirituality. All roads lead to heaven. Karma? Sure. Fate? Why not? Reincarnation?

Could be. And while you're at it, throw in a little Buddhism, Hinduism, and New Age, angel-guided living. Oprah's faith is amorphous, shape-shifting to the contours of individual preference. It's a have-it-your-way designer religion made to order for a post-Christian culture.

Oprah doesn't talk about biblical inspiration, human sinfulness, Christ's deity, substitutionary atonement, final judgment, resurrection, or hell. Why? Because they specifically define spirituality. They are truths that refute false belief systems—including the ones championed on her program.

Oprah says, "One of the biggest mistakes humans make is to believe there is only one way. Actually, there are many diverse paths leading to what you call God."[5]

Oops. Jesus didn't say, "I am *a* way and *a* truth and *a* life; I'm one way to come to the Father." He said, "I am *the* way and *the* truth and *the* life. No one comes to the Father except through me" (John 14:6, emphasis added).

Raised in a culture that condemns such thinking as narrow and intolerant, even many Christians now consider it arrogant to say that only Christians will go to heaven.

It certainly would be arrogant *if we were the ones who came up with it.* But we didn't. We're just repeating what Jesus said. We're not trusting ourselves; we're trusting Him. If it were up to us, we'd think up something more popular. But it's not up to us.

Sadly, some Christians now imagine it inappropriate to share Christ with people of other faiths. When Jews for Jesus comes to town on an evangelistic campaign, there are always Christians who say we "have no right" to be evangelizing Jews.

But let's consider that a moment.... If you see someone canoeing down rapids a hundred feet from a waterfall, getting his attention and shouting a warning may cause the canoeist some anxiety. But is smiling, waving, and keeping quiet the loving thing to do? Of course not. That would be apathy—or rank cowardice.

Going to an eternal hell isn't in anyone's best interests. How dare we, in the name of the false grace "tolerance," withhold true grace from those Jesus came to rescue?

Chapter 5

A CLOSER LOOK AT GRACE

Wesley Allan Dodd tortured, molested, and murdered three boys in Vancouver, Washington, fifteen miles from our home.

Dodd was scheduled to be hanged—the first U. S. hanging in three decades—shortly after midnight, January 4, 1993.

At dinner that evening, both our daughters, then eleven and thirteen, prayed earnestly that Dodd would repent and place his faith in Christ before he died. I agreed with their prayer...but only because I knew I should.

I stayed up and watched. Reporters from all over the country crowded around the prison. Twelve media representatives were firsthand witnesses to the execution. When they emerged thirty minutes after Dodd died, they recounted the experience.

One of them read Dodd's last words: "I had thought there was no hope and no peace. I was wrong. I have found hope and peace in the Lord Jesus Christ."

Gasps and groans erupted from the gallery. The anger was palpable. *How dare someone who has done anything so terrible say he has found hope and peace in Jesus?* Did he really think God would let him into heaven after what he'd done? *Shut up and go to hell, child killer—you won't get off so easy!*

The idea of God's offering grace to Dodd was utterly offensive.

And yet...didn't Jesus die for Dodd's sins just as He did for mine? No sin is bigger than the Savior. Grace is, literally, not of this world. I struggled with the idea of God saving Dodd only because I thought too much of myself and too little of my Lord.

I'd imagined the distance between Dodd and me as the difference between the South and North Poles. But when you consider God's viewpoint from light-years away, that distance is negligible. In my standing before a holy God, apart from Christ...I am Dodd. I am Dahmer. I am Mao.

The thought horrifies me, but it's true. It was also true of Florence Nightingale and Mother Teresa. This isn't hyperbole; it's biblical truth. Unless we come to grips with the fact that we're of precisely the same stock—fallen humanity—as Dodd and Hitler and Stalin, we'll never appreciate Christ's grace.

You say you want justice? You want Dodd and those like him to "get what's coming to them"? Be careful! Are you also willing to take what *you* have coming? There's a four-letter word for it: Hell.

My sins and yours, including our self-righteousness, nailed Jesus to that cross as surely as the sins of any child killer, terrorist, or genocidal tyrant. Let's be thankful we're not getting what we deserve!

If God isn't big enough to save Dodd and Dahmer, He's not big enough to save me.

PRESENT GRACE, FUTURE GRACE

After saying Jesus came full of grace and truth, John added, "From the fullness of his grace we have all received one blessing after another" (John 1:16). One wave after the next crashes onto the beach, before the previous wave is diminished. Thus the tide of God's grace never ceases to bring one blessing after another.

Many think of grace only in the past tense. But grace didn't end when Christ purchased our ticket out of hell.

Agencies try to trace people with large bank accounts that haven't been accessed for twenty to fifty years. The money, sometimes millions of dollars, just sits there, accumulating interest. When the legal heirs are finally discovered, they're sometimes living in absolute poverty. All along great wealth was freely accessible to them…if only they had known it.

Similarly, you and I often fail to understand how abundant the supply of grace really is. As a result, we live in spiritual poverty. We have available now all the grace we'll ever need. All we have to do is ask for it.

God's grace didn't get us going and then leave us to get by on our works. Grace didn't just justify us in the past; it sustains us in the present and will deliver us in the future. Spurgeon said:

> Our Lord Jesus is ever giving, and does not for a solitary instant withdraw his hand…the rain of His grace is always dropping, the river of His bounty is ever-flowing, and the wellspring of His love is constantly overflowing. As the King can never die, so His grace can never fail.[6]

Perhaps parents' greatest heritage to pass on to their children is the ability to perceive the multitude of God's daily blessings and to respond with continual gratitude. We should be "overflowing with thankfulness" (Colossians 2:7).

Jesus said, "Rejoice that your names are written in heaven" (Luke 10:20). If we truly grasped God's grace, even a little, we would fall on our knees and weep. Then we would get up and dance, smile, shout, and laugh, looking at each other and saying, "Can you *believe* it? We're forgiven! We're going to live forever in heaven!"

How could we do anything less?

Grace and Forgiveness

Many hear God say, "Do more" and "Do better." But not, "I've done it for you—rest." Yet this is what Jesus meant when He said, "Come to Me, all who are weary and heavy-laden.… Take My yoke upon you and learn from Me.… For My yoke is easy and My burden is light" (Matthew 11:28–30, NASB).

That's a stark contrast to the "Just try harder!" message countless Christians labor under. Many religions offer non-stop programs of self-reformation, forever walking the treadmill, putting in the miles but never finishing the work.

God invites us, "Come, all you who are thirsty, come to the waters; and you who have no money, come, buy and eat! Come, buy wine and milk without money and without cost" (Isaiah 55:1).

There's only one requirement for enjoying God's grace: being broke…and knowing it.

The Greek word *teleo* was commonly written across certificates of debt when they were canceled. It meant "paid in full." Just before Christ died, He cried out, *"Teleo"*—it is finished (John 19:30). Christ died so that the certificate of debt, listing all our sins, could once and for all be marked "paid in full."

Even though forgiveness has been offered, it's not yours until you accept it. Courts have determined that a pardon is valid only if the guilty party receives it. Christ offers each of us the gift of forgiveness, but the offer alone doesn't make it ours. To have it, we must accept it.

A friend told me he'd failed God so many times that he no longer felt worthy of God's grace. But he was never worthy in the first place! Neither am I. Grace means Christ paid our debt for us. There's nothing left for us to do but joyfully accept what He's done.

The apostle Paul himself was a murderer. Yet God not only forgave him; He elevated Paul to leadership in the church. *There are no limits to the forgiving grace of God.*

This world pours cold water onto the fires of grace and truth. As smoldering coals need each other to keep burning, we need to gather with others to celebrate Christ's grace and truth. A good church will teach you biblical truth and will also provide you with grace, acceptance, and support.[7]

Amazing Grace

Imagine a slave ship captain, a cruel Englishman who acquired slaves from Africa and transported them in slave ships to be sold like animals at auction. Imagine that this man later writes lyrics that become the most popular song of English-speaking blacks in the entire world. Unthinkable?

The song is "Amazing Grace." Some black churches sing it every Sunday. Sometimes it goes on and on, for ten or fifteen minutes. Many African-Americans love that song more than any other—even though it was written by a white man who sold black slaves and treated them like filth.

What can explain this? The same thing that explains how Christians throughout the centuries have treasured the letters of Paul, who zealously murdered Christians. It's built-in to the message:

> Amazing grace! How sweet the sound
> > that saved a wretch like me!
> I once was lost, but now am found;
> > was blind, but now I see.

The man who abused those slaves and the man who wrote that song were both named John Newton. Both shared the same DNA, but the songwriter was a new man. He became a pastor and labored to oppose the slave trade. Eighty-two years old and blind, Newton said shortly before he died, "My memory is nearly gone, but I remember two things: that I am a great sinner, and that Christ is a great Saviour."

"Amazing Grace" moves my heart more than any song I've ever heard. This hymn has been recorded more often by more musicians than any other. It can be sung at the most secular event or pagan concert, and a hush will fall on the audience. Eyes tear up. And not just the eyes of Christians.

Grace is what hearts cry out for!

Grace is what people long for, even those who don't know Jesus.

Especially those who don't know Jesus.

Chapter 6

A Closer Look at Truth

I once flew across the country to *not* preach at a church that had invited me to speak at their morning service.

After leaving my hotel, I rode to the church with a prominent Christian leader. I knew this man had been accused by the media of misrepresenting certain key details on his résumé, so I asked him about the charges.

He admitted saying and writing some things that weren't true—but it didn't seem to bother him. I told him, calmly, that I thought he should repent and publicly ask forgiveness for his dishonesty. He said nothing and we rode to the church in silence.

A few minutes after we arrived, I was escorted to the office of the senior pastor, where we were scheduled to pray together before I preached in the service. When I stepped in, the pastor slammed the door behind me. I was surprised to see his face turning scarlet, his veins bulging. He poked his finger at me. "No way will I let you preach from *my* pulpit!" he thundered.

Then out of the corner of my eye, I saw the man I had just confronted. The pastor told me I'd had no right to question our brother's integrity. The pastor was fully aware of the man's reputation but thought it none of my business. We left the office, the pastor still seething.

As the service began, the pastor took the microphone, his voice now sweet and "spiritual." He introduced the man I had confronted. This man conducted the offering, challenging the people to give generously. The pastor then addressed the church, telling them he felt "the Holy Spirit's leading" to dedicate the service to sharing and healing. Therefore, regrettably, there wouldn't be time to hear from the scheduled guest speaker—me.

On the long flight home, I marveled at how Christian leaders—who should be guardians of God's truth—could have such a blatant disregard for truth.

This isn't a new problem. "'Do not let the prophets...deceive you. Do not listen to the dreams you encourage them to have. They are prophesying lies to you in my name. I have not sent them,' declares the LORD" (Jeremiah 29:8–9).

You see, a speaker can be popular, a sermon can be greatly loved, a book can be a bestseller in Christian bookstores—and still be full of lies.

WHY TELL THE TRUTH?

Honored historians plagiarize. Politicians invent war records. Coaches embellish résumés. Employees call in sick when they're playing golf. Advertisements promise intimacy with someone beautiful if you buy this car or drink that beer.

We're so used to being lied to, and so prone to self-deceit, that it's hard to discern what's true and what's not.

Sixty-four percent of Americans say, "I will lie when it suits me if it doesn't cause any real damage." Fifty-three percent say, "I will cheat on my spouse—after all, given the chance, he or she will do the same." Only 31 percent of Americans agree that "Honesty is the best policy." When asked what they would do for 10 million dollars, 25 percent said they would abandon their family, 23 percent would become prostitutes for a week or more, and 7 percent would murder a stranger.[8]

Once we had a moral consensus. Not everybody lived by the standard, but they recognized it. The words of Judges 21:25 seem eerily prophetic of our times: "In those days there was no king in Israel; everyone did what was right in his own eyes" (NASB).

Years ago, on a family vacation, I looked into taking

my family on a boat ride. If I was willing to sit and listen to a sales presentation, we could go on the ride for fifteen dollars instead of sixty dollars.

All I had to do was sign a document claiming that I made a certain amount of money. When I explained that I didn't make that much money, the salesman said, "No problem. Just *say* you do. It's okay."

I replied that it wasn't "okay." It was a lie.

"Look," the salesman explained, "these people would rip you off in the blink of an eye. They'd lie to you in a heartbeat."

I was supposed to feel guilty—or at least incredibly stupid—for telling the truth.

I went down the street to another salesman. Children twelve and under were half price. "How old are your kids?" he asked. I said one was eleven; the other, standing there with me, was thirteen.

"No sweat," he assured me. "Just say she's twelve. They'll never know."

"But it's not true."

"What's the difference?"

"The truth matters. We're trying to teach our children that."

As we left he shook his head, muttering under his breath.

My wife's family has a cabin on the Oregon coast. Every year they have a Fourth of July parade. People on the floats and trucks throw saltwater taffy into the crowd.

One year after the parade, the streets were covered with taffy wrappers. Hundreds, everywhere. If there had been one or two, I wouldn't have noticed, but the cumulative effect was striking. That pretty little beach town had become an eyesore.

Lies are like that. They pile up. Take each lie and multiply it by tens of millions in business, school, family, and government, and you have monumental moral erosion. It's like bleeding to death from ten thousand paper cuts.

Aleksandr Solzhenitsyn said in his Nobel Prize acceptance address, "One word of truth outweighs the entire world." What did he mean? That the truth is bigger than us. Just as the Berlin Wall finally toppled, the weight of all the world's lies can be toppled by a single truth. Truth resonates in the human heart. People may resist it, yet it's the truth they need, for it's the truth that sets them free.

Tragically, Christians can be as untruthful as the world. Some Christian speakers regularly misrepresent the truth. The names of Christian celebrities are prominent on books they didn't write. Christian leaders take credit for columns written by their assistants. Christian liberal arts colleges routinely publish doctrinal statements that many faculty members neither believe nor teach. Some Christian musicians take offerings for needy children, not divulging that they retain 20 percent for themselves.

When we fail to tell the truth, we fail to represent Jesus, who is the Truth.

TRUTH ON CAMPUS?

University students, once known as truth-seekers, now have minds so "open" they don't critically evaluate truth-claims. They sit passively while professors affirm the random evolution of complex life forms. No mention is made of the biochemical discoveries of irreducible complexity at the cellular level, which refute Darwinism and constitute overwhelming scientific evidence for intelligent design.[9] Many professors are not truth-seekers, but status quo gatekeepers, highly selective about which "truths" they allow in the classroom door.

Allan Bloom said in *The Closing of the American Mind,* "There is one thing a professor can be absolutely certain of: almost every student entering the university believes, or says he believes, that truth is relative."[10]

"The really important thing (so they say) *isn't finding the truth; it's searching for it."*

Really? Try applying the same logic to your search for a job or parking space—or a flotation device when you're drowning.

"There's no such thing as truth."

Is that a true statement? Apparently it can't be. And why would anyone go to college to learn from professors who believe there is no truth?

"Truth is whatever you sincerely believe."

You can walk off a ledge sincerely believing you won't fall, but gravity cares nothing about your sincerity. We're not nearly as sincere as we imagine, but even when we are, we're often wrong.[11]

"What's true for you is true for you, and what's true for me is true for me."

So, if we step off the roof at the same time, I'll fall because I believe in gravity, but you'll hover in the air because you don't?

Such silly statements are routine on some campuses. What's even sillier is that parents and students invest vast amounts of tuition money for the privilege of hearing them.

Think about it: Is education really possible in an environment that scorns the very existence of truth? Facts can be taught, skills learned, propaganda disseminated, diplomas dispensed. But that isn't education.

In many classrooms, those who believe Scripture are routinely accused of arrogance. Jesus said God's word is truth (John 17:17). It's not arrogance to believe what the Bible teaches. It's the opposite. Arrogance is when we try to tailor truth to our preferences.

To dismiss Christ as mistaken, or the Bible as irrelevant, is the ultimate arrogance. "Anyone who does not believe God has made him out to be a liar" (1 John 5:10).

What could be more arrogant—or dangerous—than calling God a liar?

Only 22 percent of adults believe in absolute moral truths. Of those thirty-six and under, only 13 percent. Amazingly, among those who say "they know they will go to heaven after they die solely because they have confessed their sins and accepted Christ as their Savior," only 32 percent believe in absolute moral truths.[12]

Theological illiteracy and unbelief have dramatically increased among evangelical Christians in the past three decades. Churches are in desperate need of a fresh infusion of truth, a vigorous teaching of biblical doctrine. Without it, we and our children will have nothing to offer this truth-deprived world.

TRUTH AND CONSEQUENCES

My father was the most resistant person to the gospel I've ever known. He warned me never to talk to him again about "that religious stuff."

At age eighty-four, Dad was diagnosed with terminal cancer. One day he phoned, very upset.

"I've called…to say good-bye. I'm in terrible pain—I know the end's coming. I've got a gun to my head. I'm sorry to leave you with a mess."

I begged him to hold on. Jumping into my car, I made

the thirty-minute drive in twenty, rushed out of the car, and pounded on the door.

No answer.

Taking a deep breath, I opened the door. On the floor I saw a rifle and a handgun. Calling out for my father, I turned the corner into his room, prepared for the worst. Eyes half-closed, I bumped into him as he walked out. I rushed him to the hospital, where they scheduled him for surgery the next morning.

I arrived an hour before surgery, praying that in his pain and despair, with no easy way out, my dad would turn to Christ. Standing by his bed, I opened my Bible to Romans. I began reading in chapter 3. "'There is none righteous, no, not one....' All have sinned and fall short of the glory of God" (vv. 10, 23, NKJV).

Those weren't easy words to read.

My tavern-owner father had always taken hot offense at being called a sinner. I wanted to gloss over this portion, moving quickly to the good news of God's grace. But I forced myself to keep reading, verse after verse, about human sin. Why? *Because,* I told myself, *if I really love Dad, I have to tell him the whole truth. If God's going to do a miracle of conversion here, that's His job. My job is to say what God says.*

We made it to Romans 6: "The wages of sin is death, but the gift of God is eternal life in Christ Jesus our Lord"

(v. 23). Then Romans 10, about being saved through confessing Jesus as our risen Lord.

Finally I looked Dad in the eyes and asked, "Have you ever confessed your sins and asked Jesus Christ to forgive you?"

"No," he said in a weak voice. "But…I think it's about time I did."

I'll never forget that moment. The impossible took place right before my eyes: My father prayed aloud, confessed his sins, and placed his faith in Christ, just before they wheeled him into surgery. To me, dividing the Red Sea paled in comparison to this miracle.

The surgery was successful. God gave me five more precious years with my dad. The day I held his hand as he died, I knew I would see not only my mom, but also my dad in heaven.

That morning in the hospital I wanted to minimize the truth of human sin. I wanted to pass truth and go directly to grace. Yet without the bad news, there can be no good news. Without the truth of God's holiness and the stark reality of our sin, Christ's grace is meaningless.

The worst thing I could have done to my father was what I was tempted to do—water down the truth. It would have made it easier on me for the moment. But withholding God's truth from my dad would have been withholding from him God's grace.

Chapter 7

THE GRACE WE LONG FOR

The story is told of a little girl who prayed, "Lord, make the bad people good and the good people nice."

She'd probably seen adults with stern faces stare her down because she dared to fidget during a church service.

Truth without grace breeds a self-righteous legalism. People become frightened deer caught in the headlights of man-made rules. Long lists and long faces turn people from Christ.

But grace frees us from bondage and pulls the world toward Christ. Truth is good advice. Grace is good news. Good advice isn't enough. Human hearts crave good news.

My father, the tavern owner, also supplied pool tables, jukeboxes, and amusement machines for other taverns.

Dad sometimes took me with him on his route. At ten years old I'd been in more taverns than most Christians ever see in a lifetime. And to tell you the truth, I loved it. The men would ask me to shoot pool. The barmaids would invite me to sit at the bar and talk. They'd give me soda pop and corn curls. I remember thinking, *I can't wait until I'm twenty-one so I can go to taverns whenever I want.*

When I was in high school, I became a Christian and soon heard a sermon against taverns. I figured the pastor hadn't seen what I'd seen—nice, friendly people who listened to and loved each other, generous with their money and time. Most of them felt far more welcome and accepted in a bar than they ever had inside the doors of a church. Until very recently, so had I.

I'm not romanticizing taverns. But I am saying that Jesus, who had a reputation for investing time with sinners, would preach five sermons against self-righteous churches for every one against taverns!

LES MISÉRABLES

Why has Victor Hugo's *Les Misérables* been so wildly popular as a novel, play, and movie? Why do people see or read it again and again? Why does it make them weep?

Transformed by the grace of a bishop, who shields him from the consequences of his theft and assault, Jean Valjean makes a new life for himself as a businessman, mayor, and benefactor. But he's stalked relentlessly by the police detective Javert, the ultimate legalist, who is determined that the letter of the law must be carried out.

Valjean saves Javert's life. He frees the man who is his only obstacle to freedom. He releases someone who has the power to destroy him. Unable to comprehend such startling grace, Javert ends his life, restoring Valjean to freedom.

Les Misérables runs on the tracks of grace—surprising, shocking, amazing grace. Valjean is transformed by grace. Then he extends that grace to an equally unworthy man. And where did this cycle of grace begin? With the One who showed grace to the bishop who showed grace to Valjean—Jesus Christ.

Les Misérables is about the greatness of grace. Its incredible popularity should remind us how people long for Christ's grace.

THE LOST SON

Jesus tells us of the prodigal son (Luke 15:11–32). The son scorns his father, demands his inheritance, leaves home, and squanders it all in immorality. Starving, he comes back to his father to beg mercy.

How would you expect the father to respond? Refuse to let him on the property? Tell him he has been disowned? Flog him? Make him a slave? Yell at him? Lecture him? Say "I told you so"?

Jesus tells us: "But while he was still a long way off, his father saw him and was filled with compassion for him; he ran to his son, threw his arms around him and kissed him" (v. 20).

The father dresses him in the finest robe, puts a ring on his finger and sandals on his feet. He prepares the fattened calf, laying out a feast, celebrating on the grandest scale. He cries, "This son of mine was dead and is alive again; he was lost and is found" (v. 24).

Dignified men in the Middle East didn't run. And they certainly didn't throw parties for sons guilty of shame and waste.

The meaning? Our father rejoices at repentant sinners, showering us with grace.

(Just offstage there's a truth-oriented older brother who has no place for grace. Resenting his brother's reinstatement, he essentially says to his father, "Look at all I've done for you. You owe me!")

HEAVEN'S PARTY

Philip Yancey tells a modern-day version of the prodigal son, about a girl with a nose ring and an attitude. She rebels against her parents, runs away, and becomes a drug-addicted prostitute in Detroit.

The months go by. She sees her face on a milk carton but never bothers to tell her family she's alive. Then, two years later, she gets sick and desperate. Her pimp throws her out on the street.

All other alternatives exhausted, she calls home. She leaves a message on the answering machine, gets on a Greyhound, and shows up at the bus station, figuring she'll scrounge a ride to her old house.

As she steps off the bus, she finds herself greeted by forty brothers, sisters, uncles, aunts, cousins, grandparents, and her parents, all wearing party hats, with a huge banner stretched out saying, "Welcome home."

Before she can finish saying "I'm sorry," her father murmurs, "Hush, sweetheart, we'll talk later. We've got to get you home to the party; there's a banquet waiting for you!"[13]

Such abundant grace almost makes the parent look foolish, doesn't it? Looking foolish is a risk God willingly takes in extending us grace. We expect Him to extract His pound of flesh, to make us grovel and beg. But He doesn't.

Just before He told of the prodigal son, Jesus said, "There will be more rejoicing in heaven over one sinner who repents than over ninety-nine righteous persons who do not need to repent." Again, He said, *"There is rejoicing in the presence of the angels of God over one sinner who repents."*

Those in heaven see and celebrate conversions on earth. Heaven throws a party for every sinner who repents.

Sinners embracing God's grace means it's party time in heaven. And it should mean party time on earth.

GRACE VERSUS TOLERANCE

Think about the girl who ran off to Detroit. Some would blame her parents, because their standards were too high. If they'd never set a curfew, never had any rules, their daughter wouldn't have had anything to rebel against.

If she wants to watch sleazy movies, fine. If she wants to hang around kids who do drugs, okay. If she wants to sleep with her boyfriend, well, it's her life—we'll just provide her with birth control. We don't want to alienate her by being uptight or bossy.

Such parents sometimes imagine they're showing "grace" to their children. But it isn't grace at all. It's just low standards and high tolerance of sin.

Grace never lowers the standards of holiness. Jesus didn't lower the bar; He *raised* it! "You've heard that it was said, 'do not commit adultery.' I say don't look at a woman with lust" (see Matthew 5:27–28).

A home full of grace is also full of truth because grace doesn't make people less holy; it makes them *more* holy. Grace doesn't make people despise or neglect truth; it makes them love and follow truth. Far from a free pass to sin, grace is a supernatural empowerment *not* to sin (Titus 2:11–12).

Grace raises the bar, but it also enables us to joyfully jump over that bar.

Any concept of grace that leaves us—or our children—thinking that truth is unimportant is not biblical grace.

THE SELF-RIGHTEOUS

Jesus came down hardest on the very people whose doctrinal statement was the closest to His own. The Pharisees were the Bible-believing faithful of their day.

Jesus said, "Two men went up to the temple to pray, one a Pharisee and the other a tax collector. The Pharisee stood up and prayed about himself: 'God, I thank you that I am not like other men—robbers, evildoers, adulterers—or even like this tax collector. I fast twice a week and give a tenth of all I get.'"

His words drip with self-congratulation. He achieves status by comparison, elevating himself by pulling down others.

Then Jesus describes the other man: "But the tax collector stood at a distance." He felt unworthy to even stand near the temple, a place of God's holy presence. "He would not even look up to heaven, but beat his breast and said, 'God, have mercy on me, a sinner.'"

Jesus said, "I tell you that this man, rather than the other, went home justified before God" (Luke 18:9–14).

To be justified is to be declared righteous. But how can

the unrighteous be declared righteous? Paul tells us: "Abraham believed God, and it was credited to him as righteousness" (Romans 4:3). Righteousness never comes by faith in self, but by faith in God. The religious leader believed in himself, giving no mercy. The tax collector believed in God, begging for mercy.

When you boil life down to the basics, there are two kinds of people: sinners who admit their sin and sinners who deny it.

Which kind are you?

OBJECTIONS TO GRACE

During a British conference on comparative religions, scholars debated what belief, if any, was totally unique to the Christian faith.

Incarnation? The gods of other religions appeared in human form. Resurrection? Other religions tell of those returning from the dead. The debate went on until C. S. Lewis wandered into the room. The scholars posed the question to him.

"That's easy," Lewis replied. "It's grace."[14]

Our Babel-building pride insists that we must work our way to God. Only the Christian faith presents God's grace as unconditional. That so goes against our instinct, so violates our pride, that man never would have made it up. (That's a major reason Lewis believed it.)

"All religions are basically the same"? Imagine a geometry or French teacher who said to his students, "It doesn't matter what answers you give on the test. All answers are basically the same."

Hinduism's gods are many and impersonal. Christianity's God is one and personal. Buddhism offers no forgiveness or divine intervention. Christianity offers forgiveness and divine intervention. In Judaism and Islam, men earn righteous status before God through doing good works. In Christianity, men gain righteousness only by confessing their unrighteousness and being covered by Christ's merit. Every other religion is man working his way to God. Christianity is God working His way to men.

If you want a religion that makes you look good, Christianity is a poor choice. It does, however, have something wonderful going for it—it's true!

ONE CONDITION

Michael Christopher's play *The Black Angel* is about Herman Engel, a Nazi general guilty of despicable war crimes. At the Nuremberg trials he was sentenced to thirty years in prison.

When he got out he made a new beginning, building a cabin for himself and his wife in a remote part of France.

But there was a French journalist named Morrieaux, whose family had been massacred by Engel's troops. Morrieaux clung to thirty years of bitterness and was bent on revenge.

The journalist traced Engel to the French village, went into town, and stirred up hatred. The men agreed they'd go up that night and kill Engel and his wife, burning their cabin to the ground.

But that afternoon Morrieaux confronted Engel, interrogating him throughout the day. As time wore on, Morrieaux saw this tired, pathetic man's guilty and tortured soul. Revenge began to taste sour.

Finally Morrieaux said, "They're going to kill you tonight. Come with me now and I'll get you out."

Engel looked at him intently. "I will go with you on one condition."

"What condition?"

"That you forgive me."

"No," said Morrieaux. "I will save your life…but I cannot forgive you."

Engel refused to leave. That night his cabin burned to the ground. He and his wife were murdered.

Why was this forgiving grace more important to Engel than life itself? And why could Morrieaux not find it in himself to grant it? Haunting questions.

The good news is that there's a God much bigger than Engel, a Savior much bigger than Engel's sin. And there's a God much bigger than Morrieaux…much bigger than his inability to forgive.

Chapter 8

THE TRUTH THAT
SETS US FREE

John 2 highlights Christ's first miracle. Wouldn't you expect it to be something earthshaking?

So what did Jesus do for an opener? He turned water into wine. Why? So the hosts could be saved embarrassment and the people could laugh, dance, and enjoy the wedding feast. What He did was no great declaration of truth. It was just a thoughtful act of grace.

In contrast, the very next scene shows Jesus making a whip, turning over tables, and driving merchants out of the temple courts, shouting, "How dare you turn my Father's house into a market!"

Jesus was consumed with His Father's righteous standards. He wouldn't tolerate disregard for holiness and truth.

The grace of the wedding feast still in the air, what He did in the temple courtyards was a striking affirmation of truth.

Like two suns that revolve around each other to form a binary star, truth and grace are equal, essential, and inseparable. One may momentarily eclipse the other, but soon its twin emerges over the horizon to take its rightful place alongside.

In John 1, we're told Jesus came full of grace and truth. In John 2, we're given a demonstration of grace followed by a demonstration of truth. They are juxtaposed, startlingly paradoxical. Yet encompassed in the person of Jesus, they are entirely consistent.

The ancient, historical Jesus came full of grace and truth. The modern, mythological Jesus comes full of tolerance and relativism. Even in the church truth is sometimes buried under subjectivism and cowardice, while grace is lost in a sea of permissiveness and indifference.

Without truth, we lack courage to speak and convictions to speak about. Without grace, we lack compassion to meet people's deepest needs.

The vast majority of American colleges were built with the vision and funding of Christians. Why? To teach truth.

Most American hospitals were built with the vision and funding of Christians. Why? To extend grace.

We don't have the luxury of choosing either grace or truth. Yet many believers habitually embrace one instead of the other, according to our temperament, background, church, or family.

We must learn to say yes to both grace and truth—and say no to whatever keeps us from them.

NICER THAN JESUS?

The Christian life is not based on avoiding the truth but on hearing and submitting to it. The greatest kindness we can offer each other is the truth.

We've been schooled that it's inappropriate to say anything negative. Being a good witness once meant faithfully representing Christ, even when it meant being unpopular. Now it means "making people like us."

We've redefined *Christlike* to mean "nice."

By that definition, Christ wasn't always Christlike. He confronted people with sin, raised His voice, threw tables, and called people snakes, blind hypocrites, and whitewashed tombs. If we don't talk about sin and hell because we want to be nice, we're trying to be nicer than Jesus, who spoke a great deal about both.

The shifting evangelical positions on sin and hell illustrate our failure to reconcile grace and truth. While liberal groups and cults have always denied or redefined hell, evangelicals have consistently held to the biblical teaching that hell is real and eternal. Until recently.

I have an acquaintance who argues that, because he

believes in God's grace, he cannot believe in hell. He now embraces universalism. He says men cannot go to an eternal hell because Jesus purchased the world's redemption. "I love people too much to send them to hell," he says. "Surely God loves them more than I do!"

If logic were my authority, I might agree. But since Scripture's my authority (and left to myself, my logic is twisted), I can't. I asked him if he believed heaven was eternal. Yes, of course, he said. I read him Christ's words in Matthew 25:46: "Then they will go away to eternal punishment, but the righteous to eternal life." The same Greek word translated *eternal* is used of both heaven and hell. If heaven lasts forever, so does hell.

He shrugged his shoulders, then reiterated that God's grace makes eternal hell impossible. He chooses grace over hell. I believe both, because the Bible teaches both.

Jesus spoke about hell more than anyone else in Scripture. Twelve of the fourteen times the central New Testament word for *hell* is used, it's used by Jesus. He spoke of being in danger of the fire of hell (Matthew 5:22) and being thrown into hell (v. 29), asking "How will you escape being condemned to hell?" (23:33).

Ironically, the false doctrine my acquaintance advocates backfires since it removes urgency from the gospel and thereby keeps people *from* grace. His denial of hell in the name of grace discourages people from the grace he loves, while leading them toward the hell he hates and denies.

Even many who aren't universalists are lowering the stakes of redemption by denying that hell is eternal.

He who thinks he's not drowning won't reach for the life preserver. Why should he?

THE REAL QUESTION

If we were holy, we'd realize that the strange thing *isn't* why God would send people to hell. He's infinitely righteous and we're sinners, steeped in rebellion. Send people to hell? No-brainer. Where else would you send them?

The really disturbing question (if we were holy) would be, "How could a holy God send sinful men to heaven?" We ask the wrong questions because we don't grasp the truth. Therefore, we don't grasp the wonders of His grace.

We imagine that hell is out of proportion to our offenses precisely because we don't grasp how serious they are. God's grace faces hell's reality straight on, offering full deliverance. Denying hell takes the wind out of grace's sails. If there's no eternal hell, the stakes of redemption are vastly lowered. What exactly did Jesus die to rescue us from?

A rescue is only as dramatic and consequential as the fate from which someone is rescued. When people are rescued from the twentieth story of a burning building, it's heroic and newsworthy. If they're just ushered out of a smoky lobby, where's the heroism? The drama?

Grace is God's work to deliver us from the full extent of our depravity, and its full punishment. By underestimating depravity and denying eternal hell, Satan tries to lower redemption's price tag, cheapening the grace that paid the price.

Thirty years ago, many people chose churches based on whether the church believed and taught the truth. Today, many choose churches based on whether the church makes them feel comfortable. If a church tells the truth, it will gain some people but lose others.

One out of five women having an abortion in America claims to be a born-again Christian. Yet pastors tell me, "I don't talk about abortion because it will make our people feel guilty, since many have had abortions."

Isn't that exactly why we *should* talk about it? To help people—men as well as women since men are always involved—recognize and deal with their guilt and receive Christ's grace? And to help others avoid the sin that creates the guilt?

I know many women who have experienced God's forgiveness and profound healing after abortions. The women who suffer most are those who do not face the truth. Deep inside they know it, their consciences accuse them, and they pursue self-destructive behaviors. Our silence isn't grace—it's cruelty.

Ephesians 4:15 tells us to speak the truth in love, not to withhold the truth in love. Our job is not simply to help each other feel good, but to help each other *be* good.

At a time when many churches are backing away from truth-telling and discipline, secular recovery advocates are embracing truth-telling through interventions with addicts. Instead of looking the other way, they're lovingly yet firmly presenting the truth, even when uninvited. Why this move to truth-telling? Simply because *it works.*

The way to no longer feel guilty is not to deny guilt, but to face it and ask God's forgiveness.

Sometimes showing grace requires silence. Other times it requires speaking up. Your friend whose father is dying may be terrified to share Christ with him. Yet to do so is clearly in his best interests and his father's. Share the truth; then offer him grace and help. Go with him if he needs your support. Likewise, if you see a friend making poor parenting choices that may result in later grief, you owe him the truth.

Unfortunately, many nonbelievers know only two kinds of Christians: those who speak the truth without grace and those who are very nice but never share the truth. What they need to see is a third type of Christian—one who, in a spirit of grace, loves them enough to tell them the truth.

Chapter 9

GRACE AND
TRUTH TOGETHER

In the 1930s, German church leaders defended Adolf Hitler as a leader who didn't smoke or drink, encouraged women to dress modestly, and opposed pornography.

If that's your checklist, Hitler was a swell guy.

Whenever we judge righteousness by externals, we get into trouble. The Pharisees had it together on the outside. They used truth to elevate themselves while lowering everyone else.

Think everything wrong with the world is someone else's fault? Enjoy playing the blame game? Truth without grace breeds anger and cynicism. Nothing's colder than dead, legalistic orthodoxy.

Jesus acknowledged that some truths are more important than others. Loving God is first, loving your neighbor second (Matthew 22:37–39). It's not about earrings, tattoos, clothing, drinking wine, or smoking cigars. It's about justice, righteousness, love, and mercy. It's about grace and truth.

Remember Margaret Holder, who told us about "Uncle Eric"? She shared another story. The children played basketball, rounders, and hockey. Eric Liddell was their referee. Not surprisingly, he refused to referee on Sundays. But in his absence, the children fought. Liddell struggled over this. He believed he shouldn't stop the children from playing because they needed the diversion.

Finally, Liddell decided to referee on Sundays. This made a deep impression on Margaret—she saw that the athlete world famous for sacrificing success for principle was not a legalist. When it came to his own glory, Liddell would surrender it all rather than run on Sunday. But when it came to the good of children in a prison camp, he would referee on Sunday.

Liddell would sacrifice a gold medal for himself in the name of truth but would bend over backward for others in the name of grace.

POLITICAL GRACE AND TRUTH

Often, conservatives emphasize truth (morals), and liberals emphasize grace (compassion). Conservatives want to conserve what's right; liberals want to liberate from what's wrong.

Liberals' commitment to fighting racism in the sixties was commendable. But sometimes liberals fight against true standards, like the beliefs that abortion, fornication, adultery, and homosexual behavior are wrong. They embrace tolerance as a grace substitute. Liberal Christians often end up being liberals first, Christians second.

Conservatives want to restore lost values. They want to go back to the days when prayer was allowed in schools. But they forget that the same schools that allowed prayer didn't allow black children! By trying to conserve so many things—even things that were clearly wrong—conservative Christians have sometimes been conservatives first, Christians second.

Why should we have to choose between conservatism's emphasis on truth and liberalism's emphasis on grace? Why can't we oppose injustice to minorities *and* to the unborn? Why can't we oppose greedy ruination of the environment *and* anti-industry New Age environmentalism? Why can't we affirm the biblical right to the ownership of property *and* emphasize God's call to voluntarily share wealth with the needy? Why can't we uphold God's condemnation of sexual immorality, including homosexual practices, *and* reach out in love and compassion to those trapped in destructive lifestyles and dying from AIDS?

We cannot do these things if we are first and foremost either liberals or conservatives. We can do these things only if we are first and foremost followers of Christ, who is full of grace *and* truth.

SCANDALOUS GRACE

Remember George, the university professor I drove home from that theater parking lot? When we met again several months later, two hours before he came to Christ, he said, "I can't get past the idea that someone could live a selfish, no-good life, then repent on his deathbed and go to heaven. It just sounds too easy, too cheap."

I challenged his underlying assumption, that we can earn heaven. We discussed the hardest part about grace—swallowing our pride and saying, "I don't deserve this any more than that criminal does."

Grace was enormously expensive for God. Yet there's just nothing we can offer to pay for it.

A thief on the cross asked Jesus to save him. Though every spoken word was agony, Jesus answered him, "I tell you the truth, today you will be with me in paradise" (Luke 23:43).

This thief would never be baptized, make restitution, attend church, take communion, sing a hymn, or give an offering. He had nothing to offer Christ, no way to pay Him back.

Neither do we.

Remember the king who invites you to come live in his

house and be his heir, even though you rebelled against him and murdered his son? Suppose you worked hard, saved up money, then came to the king and said, "Here. I'm paying you back."

Imagine the king's response. You couldn't *begin* to pay him back. The very attempt is an insult. It cheapens his son's death.

On the other hand, some people take advantage of grace, reducing it to an excuse for sin. Jude writes: "For certain men whose condemnation was written about long ago have secretly slipped in among you. They are godless men, *who change the grace of our God into a license for immorality*" (Jude 1:4, emphasis added).

Any concept of grace that makes us feel more comfortable about sinning is not biblical grace. God's grace never encourages us to live in sin; on the contrary, it empowers us to say no to sin and yes to truth. It's the polar opposite of what Dietrich Bonhoeffer called "cheap grace."

God has seen us at our worst and still loves us. No skeletons will fall out of our closets in eternity. God won't say, "Well, if I'd known *that*, I never would've let Randy into heaven!"

God knows all my sins.

Right down to the dregs.

And Jesus died for every one of them. No exceptions.

BETTER THAN I DESERVE

We're so used to being lied to that we're suspicious of the gospel—like it's too good to be true. You know: "There's no such thing as a free lunch."

"What's the catch?"

There is none!

"Let us then *approach the throne of grace with confidence,* so that we may receive mercy and find grace to help us in our time of need" (Hebrews 4:16, emphasis added). To a devout Jew, the notion of unhindered access to God is scandalous. Yet that access is ours, freely. Because of Christ's work, God's door is always open to us.

True grace undercuts not only self-righteousness, but also self-sufficiency. God often brings us to a point where we have no place to turn but to Him. As with manna, He always gives us enough but not too much. He doesn't let us store up grace. We have to go back for it, fresh, every day, every hour.

Whenever I ask, "How are you doing?" my friend C. J. responds, "Better than I deserve."

It's not just a cute remark. He means it. And he's right. We don't deserve God's daily graces, big or small.

The Roman centurion sent word to Jesus: "I do not deserve to have you come under my roof.… I did not even consider myself worthy to come to you" (Luke 7:6–7).

Living by grace means affirming daily our unworthiness. We are never thankful for what we think we deserve. *We are deeply thankful for what we know we don't deserve.*

When you know you deserve eternal hell, it's a paradigm shift. If you realize you're undeserving, suddenly the world comes alive—you're surprised and grateful at God's many kindnesses that were invisible when you thought you deserved better. Instead of drowning in self-pity, you're floating on a sea of gratitude.

When I sense that I'm unworthy—and I often do—I'm sensing the truth. I don't need you to talk me out of my unworthiness. I need you to talk me into humbly setting it before Christ and asking Him to empower me. Yes, I cling to the reality that I'm a new person, covered in Christ's righteousness (2 Corinthians 5:17–21). But the same Paul who told us that also said, "I am less than the least of all God's people" (Ephesians 3:8).

Pride is a heavy burden. There is nothing like that feeling of lightness when God graciously lifts our self-illusions from our shoulders. Even refusing to forgive ourselves is an act of pride—it's making ourselves and our sins bigger than God and His grace.

Are we trying to atone for our sins? We can't. Only Jesus can, and He already did.

Don't try to repeat the atonement—just accept it!

Embrace God's forgiveness.

Relax.

Rejoice.

EXTENDING GRACE TO OTHERS

Jesus told of a servant whose debt to his master was ten thousand talents, the equivalent of millions of dollars. The servant begged forgiveness. Though the master had every right to imprison him for the rest of his life, he offered a full pardon.

Then this servant went out and found a fellow servant, who owed him a much smaller amount—1/600,000 of what he'd been forgiven.

He demanded full and immediate payment. The debtor fell to his knees and pleaded for mercy. But he showed no mercy, throwing him into prison.

When the master heard about this, he said, in essence, "Had my forgiveness really touched your heart, you would have extended it to your brother." The master withdrew forgiveness, since a man who won't extend grace shows an utter disregard for grace.

This parable teaches:

- Our debt to God is infinitely beyond our capacity to pay.
- Our debt to God is infinitely greater than any person's debt to us.
- When we truly experience God's forgiveness for our sins, we will be transformed into forgiving people.

"But how can I forgive my father for abusing me, my ex-wife for betraying me, my business partner for cheating me? That would take a miracle."

Exactly. Grace is that miracle.

"Do you expect me to pretend he didn't do those terrible things to me?" Not at all. God doesn't pretend we didn't do all those terrible things to Him. He doesn't pretend the nails in His hands didn't hurt.

He says, "I died to forgive you…and to give you grace to forgive others."

Extending grace frees us from the terrible burden of resentment and bitterness. Bad as they may be, anyone's offenses against me are far less than my offenses against God. If He's forgiven me, by His grace I can forgive them.

God's grace to us is lightning. Our grace to others is thunder. Lightning comes first; thunder responds. We show grace to others because He first showed grace to us.

GO AND SIN NO MORE

The truth-only crowd, the Pharisees, was ready to stone a woman for adultery (John 8:1–11). Had grace-only folks been there, they would have patted her hand and said, "Don't worry about an affair, dear. God understands, and so do we."

Jesus rebuked the woman's accusers. But that isn't the end of the story. He could have said,

"Go burn for your sins."

or

"Go and feel free to sin some more."

What He did say was, "Go and sin no more."

Jesus didn't deny truth. He affirmed it. She needed to repent. And change.

Jesus didn't deny grace. He offered it. He sent her away, forgiven and cleansed, to a new life.

Grace-only folk don't understand why Jesus said, "Fear him…who has power to throw you into hell" (Luke 12:5). Truth-only folk don't understand why Jesus hung out with sinners, and why He hung on a cross for them.

Instead of the world's apathy and tolerance, we offer grace. Instead of the world's relativism and deception, we offer truth.

If we minimize grace, the world sees no hope for salvation. If we minimize truth, the world sees no need for salvation. To show the world Jesus, we must offer unabridged grace and truth, emphasizing both, apologizing for neither. The Colossian church "understood God's grace in all its truth" (Colossians 1:6).

Truth is quick to post warning signs and guardrails at the top of the cliff. Yet it fails to empower people to drive safely—and neglects to help them when they crash.

Grace is quick to post ambulances and paramedics at the bottom of the cliff. But without truth, it fails to post warning signs and build guardrails. In so doing, it encourages the very self-destruction it attempts to heal.

Truth without grace crushes people and ceases to be truth. Grace without truth deceives people and ceases to be grace.

Truth without grace degenerates into judgmental legalism. Grace without truth degenerates into deceitful tolerance.

Christ's heart is equally grieved by grace-suppression and truth-suppression, by grace-twisting and truth-twisting.

Grace and truth are both necessary. Neither is sufficient.

We need to examine ourselves and correct ourselves. We who are truth-oriented need to go out of our way to affirm grace. We who are grace-oriented need to go out of our way to affirm truth.

"Hate the sin, but love the sinner." No one did either like Jesus.

Truth hates sin. Grace loves sinners.

Those full of grace and truth do both.

CONCLUSION

I know what it's like to be rescued.

I'd spoken at a missionary conference in Palmer, Alaska. Afterward, we were headed north to Galena by small plane. My ten-year-old, Karina, and I were flying with our missionary friend, Barry Arnold, and his daughter, Andrea. Nanci and our daughter Angie were leaving with the rest of Barry's family an hour later in another plane, taking a different route.

Well into the flight we were cruising over a beautiful waterfall at three thousand feet, when suddenly the engine lost power. Smoke billowed, oil splashed on the windshield. Seeing that there was no oil pressure, Barry had to shut off the engine, which looked like it was about to burn. Suddenly we were descending rapidly in a rough mountain pass where there was no place to land. It looked like we wouldn't make it.

By God's grace, Barry spotted just the right strip of dirt and dodged the rocks in a beautiful emergency landing. Had we been only a few miles farther, there would have been nowhere to land. We would have crashed.

We landed at 4:30 P.M. Barry set off the emergency locator transmitter and tried to reach help with the radio. We put rocks out to form an SOS, set up shelter, ate C rations, and prayed for our families, who would soon realize we were down but wouldn't know we were alive. Then we waited, hoping and praying we'd be rescued before the cold night came upon us.

In the next hours we saw three planes. Two were commercial flights, flying high. They weren't listening to the emergency frequency, didn't see our SOS or fire, and didn't notice us waving white flags. The third airplane could have seen us, but the pilot wasn't looking.

It got darker. We prepared to spend the night.

At 10:30 P.M. a search and rescue plane saw our flare. After we'd been seven hours on the ground, near midnight, a huge craft descended from above, bright lights piercing the darkness. It was a search and rescue helicopter.

The pilot got out and flashed his broad grin. He was the most welcome sight we'd ever seen. He said, "We expected wreckage. We didn't think you'd be alive."

We found out later there were four airplanes and two helicopters combing the mountains looking for us. Otherwise, we'd never have been found.

I still remember the squeals of delight from our ten-year-old girls as that helicopter with its powerful searchlight and deafening roar landed only forty feet from us. I'll never forget the sense of wonder and gratitude. When they took us on board and flew us to spend the night in a hunting lodge, it was an indescribable feeling.

I know what it means to be unable to make it out on my own. I know what it means to be overlooked by those unaware of our plight. And I know what it is to be found by someone searching, someone with resources we didn't have but desperately needed.

We would have done much better in the Alaskan wilderness without our rescuers than any of us can do without God. Left to ourselves, we're utterly helpless and hopeless. We can't lift a finger on our own behalf. We're lost in sin's wilderness, stranded, trapped in a remote ravine. No one can hear us. There's no way out. Left to ourselves, we'll die.

Unless someone comes down from above, to rescue us.

That's our only hope. And that's the gospel—God heard our cries; He searched for us, found us, and paid the ultimate price to deliver us.

This—and nothing less—is true grace.

In Jesus, "mercy and truth have met together" (Psalm

85:10, NKJV). Grace and truth met face to face on the Cross.

The grace and truth paradox is also a paradigm—a way of looking at life. People need the directions of truth to know where to go. Then they need the empowerment of grace to help them get there.

The world is weary of all the counterfeit Christs made in the image of grace-despising and truth-despising hearts. People thirst for the real Jesus. Nothing less can satisfy.

Grace and truth are His fingerprints.

We show people Jesus only when we show them grace and truth.

Anything less than both is neither.

The author and
Eternal Perspective Ministries
can be reached at www.epm.org;
39085 Pioneer Blvd., Suite 206
Sandy, OR 97055
503-668-5200
www.randyalcorn.blogspot.com

Notes

1. C. S. Lewis, *The Lion, the Witch and the Wardrobe* (New York: Scholastic, 1995), 80.
2. C. S. Lewis, *The Voyage of the Dawn Treader* (New York: Collier Books, 1970), 214–5.
3. C. S. Lewis, *Mere Christianity* (New York: Collier Books, 1960), vii.
4. Charles Spurgeon, *Morning and Evening* (Geanies House, Fearn, Scotland: Christian Focus Publications Ltd., 1994), Morning April 5.
5. As quoted by LaTonya Taylor, "The Church of O," *Christianity Today*, 1 April 2002, 45.
6. Spurgeon, *Morning and Evening*, Morning May 16.
7. If you are looking for such a church in your area but can't find one, contact our organization and if we can make some recommendations, we will: 503-663-6481 or info@epm.org.
8. James Patterson and Peter Kim, *The Day America Told the Truth* (New York: Prentice Hall Press, 1991), 25–6, 49, 66.
9. See Michael Behe, *Darwin's Black Box* (New York: The Free Press, 1996); William Dembski, *Intelligent Design* (Downers Grove, Ill.: InterVarsity Press, 1999).
10. Allan Bloom, *The Closing of the American Mind* (New York: Harcourt, Brace, 1963), 156.
11. J. Budziszewski, *How to Stay Christian in College* (Colorado Springs, Colo.: NavPress, 1999), 68–78.
12. "How America's Faith Has Changed Since 9-11," *Barna Research Online*, 26 November 2001. http://www.barna.org/cgi-bin/PagePressRelease.asp?PressReleaseID=102&Reference=D (accessed 24 September 2002).
13. Adapted from Philip Yancey, *What's So Amazing about Grace?* (Grand Rapids, Mich.: Zondervan Publishers, 1997), 49–51.
14. Ibid., 45.

Fiction
from Randy Alcorn

DECEPTION
Homicide detective Ollie Chandler has seen it all. But when he's called to investigate the murder of a Portland State University professor, all the evidence is pointing to one horrific conclusion: The murderer is someone in his own department.

DOMINION
When two murders drag a columnist into the world of gangs and racial conflict, he seeks revenge for the killings, and answers to the hard issues regarding race and faith.

DEADLINE
After tragedy strikes those closest to him, journalist Jake Woods is drawn into a complex murder investigation that forces him to ultimately seek answers to the meaning of his existence.

THE ISHBANE CONSPIRACY
Four college students have worse troubles than midterms to contend with: A demonic contingent is after their souls.

LORD FOULGRIN'S LETTERS
Lord Foulgrin's Letters invites believers to eavesdrop on their worst Enemy, learn his strategies and tricks, and discover how to ward off his devilish attacks.

OTHER BOOKS BY RANDY ALCORN

NONFICTION
Heaven
50 Days of Heaven
TouchPoints: Heaven
In Light of Eternity
Money, Possessions, and Eternity
The Law of Rewards
ProLife Answers to ProChoice Arguments
Restoring Sexual Sanity
Sexual Temptation
The Grace and Truth Paradox
The Purity Principle
The Treasure Principle
Women Under Stress
Why ProLife?
If God is Good...

FICTION
Deadline
Dominion
Deception
Edge of Eternity
Lord Foulgrin's Letters
The Ishbane Conspiracy (with Karina Alcorn and Angela Alcorn)
Safely Home

CHILDREN'S BOOKS
Heaven for Kids
Tell Me About Heaven
Wait Until Then